SCHIRMER'S LIBRARY
OF MUSICAL CLASSICS

Vol. 2116

PYOTR IL'YICH TCHAIKOVSKY

Piano Collection

Album for the Young
The Seasons
The Nutcracker Suite
8 Other Selected Piano Pieces

ISBN 978-1-4950-0454-4

G. SCHIRMER, Inc.

DISTRIBUTED BY

HAL•LEONARD®
CORPORATION
7777 W. BLUEMOUND RD. P.O. BOX 13819 MILWAUKEE, WI 53213

www.musicsalesclassical.com
www.halleonard.com

CONTENTS

THE SEASONS, OP. 37B

OTHER SELECTED PIANO PIECES

Pyotr Il'Yich Tchaikovsky
(1840–1893)

Pyotr Il'yich Tchaikovsky is regarded as the most important Russian composer of the nineteenth century. Tchaikovsky combined Russian folksong, timbres, and modes with Western form and harmonization, creating works that epitomize Russian romanticism. Many of them count among the most recognizable pieces in classical music, including *The Nutcracker*, the love theme from *Romeo and Juliet*, the opening to his Piano Concerto No. 1, and the *1812 Overture*.

Tchaikovsky was born in the small town of Votkinsk. His family moved multiple times during the first ten years of his life, first to Moscow, then to St. Petersburg, and finally to Alapayevsk, a town smaller and more remote than Votkinsk. He was able to read in French and German by the age of six, and he wrote poetry in French in addition to taking voice and piano lessons. At twelve, Tchaikovsky moved to St. Petersburg to attend the School of Jurisprudence, from which he graduated in 1859.

He took a job at the Ministry of Justice where he excelled, receiving three promotions in eight months. In the evenings, Tchaikovsky often attended the French theatre and ballet, as well as the Italian opera. He was also able to travel around the European continent on business, broadening his international perspective beyond book learning. This period in Tchaikovsky's life coincided with the rise of bourgeois music institutions, including the founding of The Russian Musical Society in 1859, which organized concerts and provided music classes to the general public. Tchaikovsky began taking music theory lessons given by the society in 1861, and in 1862 he began formal music studies at the St. Petersburg Conservatory in its inaugural semester. Tchaikovsky flourished at the conservatory, maturing rapidly as a composer under Anton Rubinstein while also studying theory, piano, flute, and organ.

Tchaikovsky graduated in 1865 and moved to Moscow to teach theory at the Moscow Conservatory. He had been recommended for the job by Nikolay Rubinstein, Anton's brother. Rubinstein was a co-founder of both the Moscow Conservatory and the Moscow branch of the Russian Musical Society. He made sure that the society's orchestra was at Tchaikovsky's disposal and he also premiered many of Tchaikovsky's piano works, ensuring that Moscow's audiences would have ample opportunity to hear the young composer's music.

In 1877, Tchaikovsky left the conservatory and gained financial independence through the help of a wealthy widow, Nadezhda von Meck. He would eventually serve as director of the Moscow chapter of the Russian Musical Society, and in 1888 he was awarded a lifetime pension from the Emperor Alexander III. Tchaikovsky died in October 1893, one week after conducting the premiere of his Sixth Symphony, of unknown causes.

Tchaikovsky's oeuvre covers all the major genres, including symphonies, program music, string quartets, piano works, instrumental concertos, songs, operas, and ballets. He admired French music, but was perhaps more influenced by Beethoven, Schubert, and Schumann, in addition to the use of timbres in orchestral writing by his Russian predecessors such as Glinka. He differed from his well-established Russian contemporaries who made up the composer consortium known as The Five. This group, which included Balakirev, Borodin, Cui, Mussorgsky, and Rimsky-Korsakov, had a nationalistic bent that caused them to shy away from the more Western models that Tchaikovsky embraced. Tchaikovsky set himself apart through a combination of idiosyncratic aspects of Russian music, sublimely emotional melodic writing, and Western European genres and forms. This allowed his music to appeal to a broader international audience, and it continues to bring joy to audiences and musicians around the world.

Album for the Young
Opus 39

ALBUM FOR THE YOUNG

1. Morning Prayer

Pyotr Il'yich Tchaikovsky
Op. 39

2. A Winter Morning

3. The Hobby Horse

4. Mamma

12

5. March of the Tin Soldiers

6. The Sick Doll

7. The Doll's Burial

8. Waltz

9. The New Doll

10. Mazurka

11. Russian Song

12. The Peasant Plays the Accordion

13. Folk Song

14. Polka

15. Italian Song

16. Old French Song

17. German Song

18. Neapolitan Dance Song

19. The Nurse's Tale

20. The Witch

21. Sweet Dreams

22. Song of the Lark

23. The Organ Grinder

24. In Church

The Nutcracker Suite

Opus 71a

THE NUTCRACKER SUITE
Miniature Overture

Arranged by Stepán Esipoff
Edited by Carl Deis

Pyotr Il'yich Tchaikovsky
Op. 71a

March

Tempo di Marcia vivo

Dance of the Sugar Plum Fairy

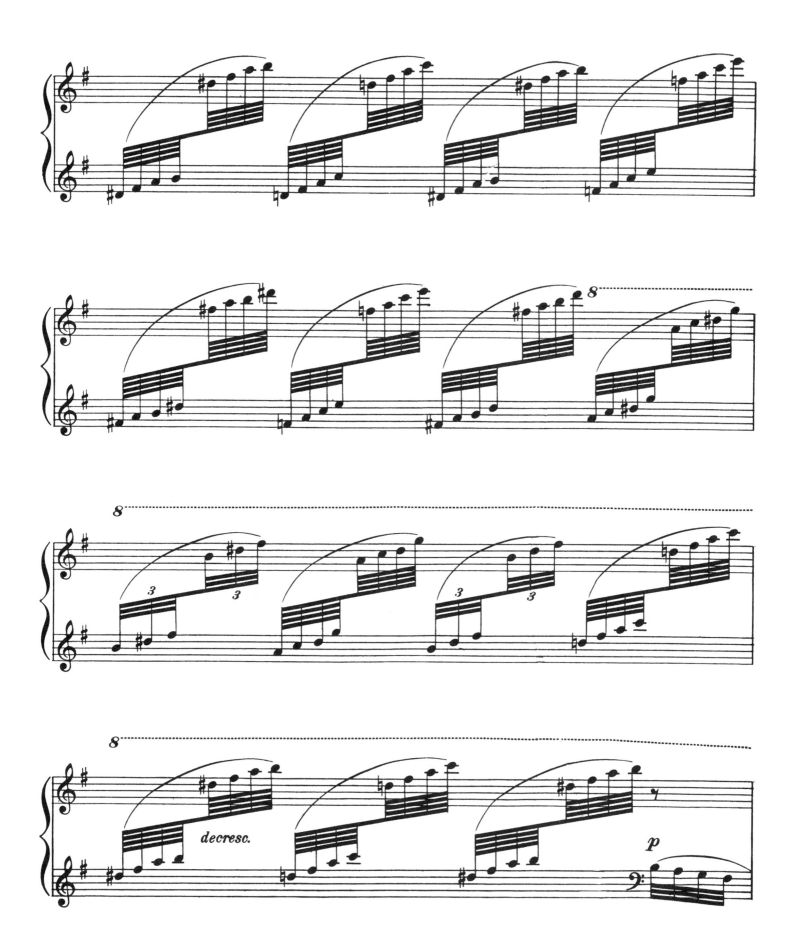

Russian Dance, "Trepak"

Tempo di Trepak, molto vivace

Arabian Dance

Chinese Dance

Dance of the Reed Flutes

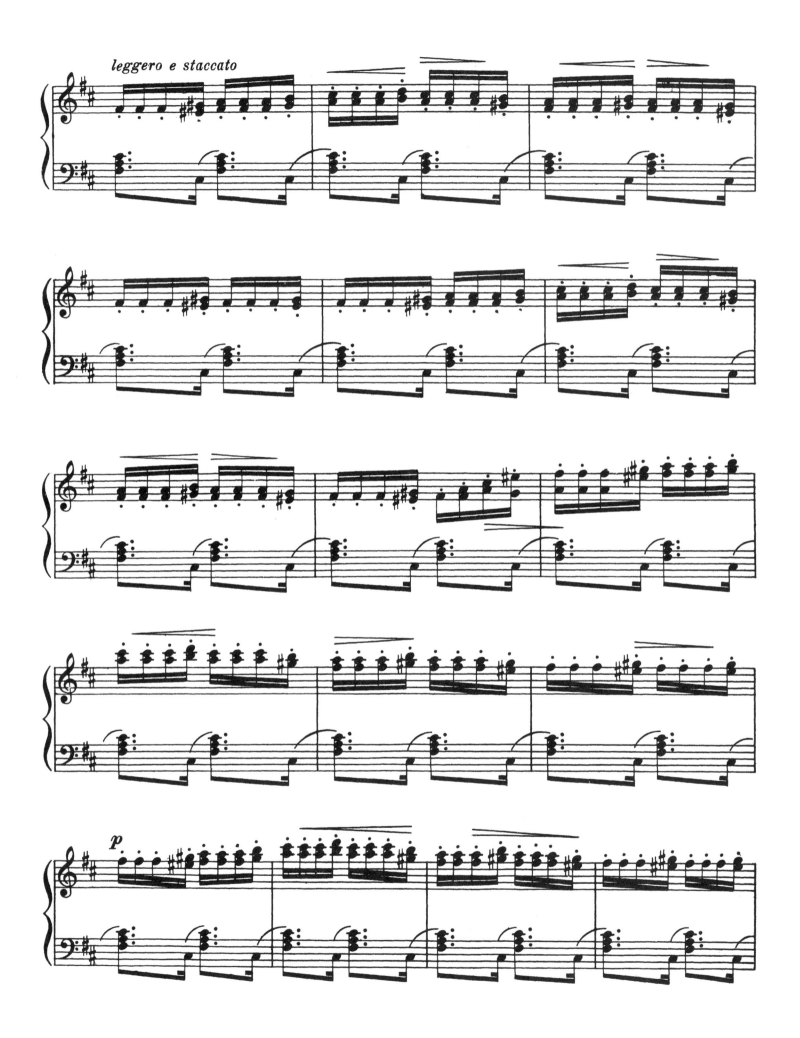

Waltz of the Flowers

THE SEASONS
OPUS 37B

JANUARY
By the Hearth

Edited and fingered by
Louis Oesterle

Pyotr Il'yich Tchaikovsky
Op. 37a

FEBRUARY
Carnival

L'istesso tempo

MARCH

Song of the Lark

APRIL
Snowdrop

Edited and fingered by
Louis Oesterle

MAY
Starlit Night

JUNE
Barcarolle

Edited and fingered by
Louis Oesterle

JULY
Song of the Reaper

AUGUST
Harvest Song

SEPTEMBER
Hunter's Song

Allegro non troppo

OCTOBER
Autumn Song

Andante doloroso e molto cantabile

NOVEMBER
Troika

DECEMBER
Christmas

OTHER SELECTED PIANO PIECES
FROM OPUSES 2, 5, 10, 19, AND 40

RÊVERIE DU SOIR

Edited and fingered by
Louis Oesterle

Pyotr Il'yich Tchaikovsky
Op. 19, No. 1

L'istesso tempo.

Fine.

CHANT SANS PAROLES

Pyotr Il'yich Tchaikovsky
Op. 2, No 3

Allegretto grazioso e cantabile.

ROMANCE

Pyotr Il'yich Tchaikovsky
Op. 5

Andante cantabile

Allegro energico.

NOCTURNE

Pyotr Il'yich Tchaikovsky
Op. 10, No. 1

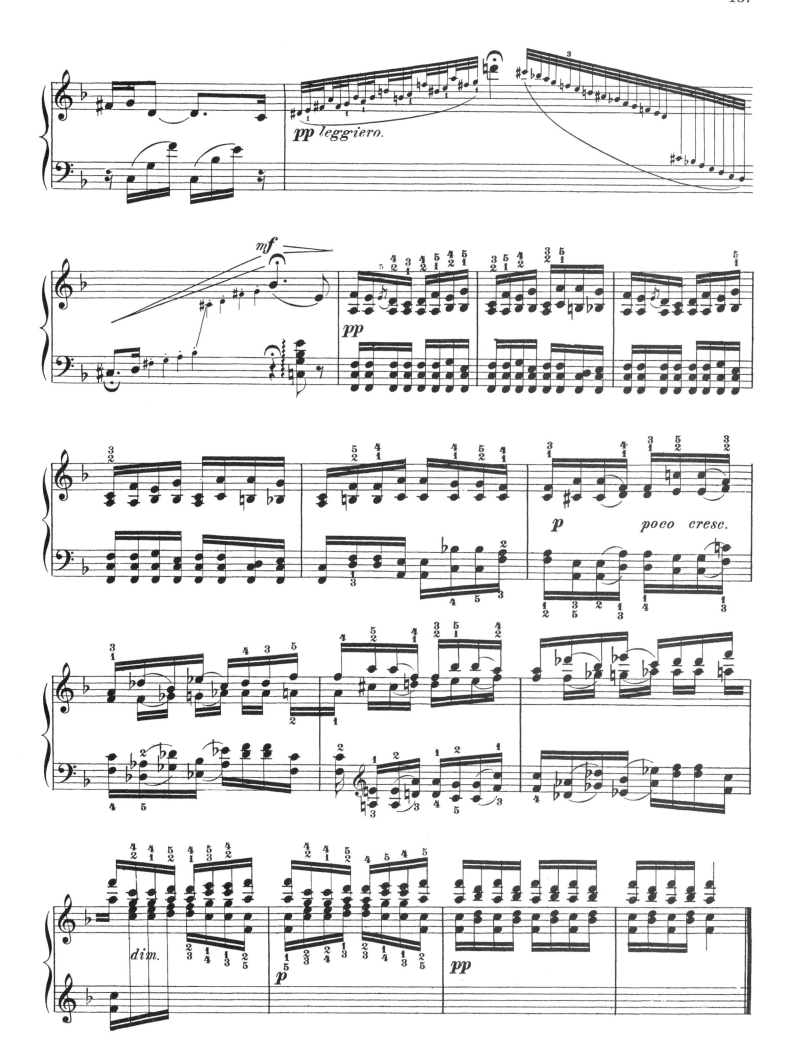

HUMORESQUE

Pyotr Il'yich Tchaikovsky
Op. 10, No. 2

FEUILLET D'ALBUM

Pyotr Il'yich Tchaikovsky
Op. 19, No. 3

Allegretto semplice

CHANSON TRISTE

Edited and fingered by
W. K. Bassford

Pyotr Il'yich Tchaikovsky
Op. 40, No. 2

Allegro non troppo

la melodia con molta espressione

CHANT SANS PAROLES

Pyotr Il'yich Tchaikovsky
Op. 40, No. 6

Allegro moderato